UNMASKING INCOME TAX MYTHS

Bringing Clarity to Salaried and Small Business Owners

BY

CA RITESH PAL

★ ★ ★

CA Ritesh Pal, B.Com, M.Com, LL.B., FCA, is a seasoned Chartered Accountant with over a decade of experience in finance, taxation, and business advisory. Since 2015, he has been practicing independently, serving a diverse clientele that includes startups, MSMEs, professionals, and individuals.

He holds a prestigious **Certificate in Forensic Accounting and Fraud Detection** from the Institute of Chartered Accountants of India (ICAI), adding an investigative dimension to his already extensive financial expertise.

Ritesh specializes in **direct and indirect taxation, startup compliance, business registrations, and strategic financial planning**. Known for simplifying complex tax laws and regulatory processes, he has earned the trust of small business owners and entrepreneurs as a reliable and insightful advisor.

Beyond his practice, Ritesh is a **regular speaker at business forums** and a **guest lecturer at colleges and universities**, where he shares practical insights and empowers the next generation of finance professionals.

Driven by a passion for financial literacy and client success, **CA Ritesh Pal** continues to make a meaningful impact in the financial and entrepreneurial community.

Unmasking Income Tax Myths is a practical and eye-opening guide designed to break down the misconceptions surrounding India's income tax laws.

Written in a clear, jargon-free style by experienced Chartered Accountant **CA Ritesh Pal**, this book is a must-read for salaried individuals, small business owners, professionals, and startup founders who want to understand the truth behind the most common tax myths.

This book addresses everything from the fear of income tax notices to confusion around deductions, exemptions, and audits. Each chapter blends real-world examples with simplified explanations, helping readers separate fact from fiction and make informed financial decisions.

Whether you're filing your returns, planning your taxes, or simply looking to get a better grasp of how the Indian tax system actually works, this book will equip you with the clarity and confidence you need.

Unmasking Income Tax Myths is not just about saving taxes—it's about **empowering you with the knowledge to stay compliant, confident, and financially smart.**

Who Is This Book For? 

This book is written for the **dreamers, doers, and builders**—the small business owners, startup founders, freelancers, and self-employed professionals who are navigating the world of income tax with uncertainty, confusion, or maybe even a little fear.

If you've ever believed that:

- "Small businesses don't need to worry about income tax."

- "Cash transactions are off the radar."

- "Only big companies get audited."

- or "My CA will handle everything, I don't need to know the rules"—

Then this book is for **you**.

Unmasking Income Tax Myths is not a textbook. It's a **real-world guide** designed to clear the fog around common misconceptions, give you clarity on your obligations, and help you make smarter decisions without relying entirely on hearsay or half-baked advice.

Whether you're just starting up, scaling your business, or trying to get compliant after years of confusion, this book will empower you with practical knowledge, straightforward explanations, and a confident understanding of how India's income tax system really works for businesses like yours.

ACKNOWLEDGMENT 

Writing this book has been a journey of learning, reflection, and purpose—and it wouldn't have been possible without the support and inspiration of some truly special people in my life.

First and foremost, I express my deepest gratitude to all my **mentors**—the guiding lights who have shaped my thinking, sharpened my skills, and encouraged me to pursue clarity and truth in every professional endeavor.

Your wisdom and generosity have left a lasting impact on both my career and this book.

To my **wife, Priyanka**—your unwavering belief in me, your patience during the long writing hours, and your constant encouragement kept me grounded and focused. You are my strongest pillar, and I am deeply thankful for your love and support.

And to my lovely daughter, **Aanya**—you are my brightest inspiration. Your curiosity, innocence, and pure joy remind me every day of the importance of honesty, simplicity, and clarity— values I've tried to bring into these pages.

This book is, in many ways, written with you in my heart.

Thank you to every reader who chooses to pick up this book. May it bring you the clarity and confidence you deserve.

With gratitude,

CA Ritesh Pal

DISCLAIMER 

The information provided in this book is intended solely for general guidance and educational purposes. While every effort has been made to ensure the accuracy and reliability of the content, the author does not warrant or guarantee the completeness or correctness of the information contained herein.

Income tax laws are subject to change, and the interpretation of tax laws can vary based on specific circumstances, legal precedents, and evolving government regulations. The content of this book is based on current laws and practices at the time of publication. Readers are strongly encouraged to consult with a qualified Chartered Accountant or tax professional for advice tailored to their specific situation before making any financial or tax-related decisions.

The author and publisher disclaim any liability or responsibility for any errors, omissions, or damages arising from the use of this book's content.

TABLE OF CONTENTS

WHY SHOULD I PAY TAXES?

Taxes are often perceived as an obligation, a financial burden imposed by the government. However, in reality, taxes are the foundation of a nation's progress and prosperity. Every rupee paid as Tax contributes to building roads, enhancing national security, improving healthcare, and uplifting the underprivileged.

Paying taxes is not merely a legal duty; it is a civic responsibility that fuels the development of the country. The government uses the Tax for:

Building Infrastructure and Public Services

Strong infrastructure is the backbone of any developed nation. Taxes fund the highways we travel on, the bridges we cross, and the railways that connect distant regions. Taxes also support public services such as fire departments, disaster management, and waste disposal systems, ensuring a safer and cleaner environment for all citizens.

The Delhi-Mumbai Expressway, one of India's largest highway projects, is financed through public funds, including taxes. Similarly, metro expansions in cities like Bengaluru, Mumbai, and Chennai are made possible through tax revenue.

Funding Government Schemes and Social Welfare Programs

Taxes serve as the financial backbone of various government welfare schemes aimed at improving the quality of life for millions.

From healthcare and employment programs to financial inclusion initiatives, taxes help bridge the gap between economic disparity and social well-being.

Here are a few schemes:-

- **Pradhan Mantri Jan Dhan Yojana:** Enables financial inclusion by providing banking access to the unbanked.

- **Ayushman Bharat:** Offers free healthcare to low-income families.

- **MGNREGA:** Ensures rural employment and livelihood security.

- **PM Kisan Samman Nidhi Yojana:** Provides financial assistance to farmers.

Strengthening National Security and Defence

A strong and well-equipped defense system is essential for national sovereignty and safety. The government utilizes tax revenue to maintain and upgrade the Indian Army, Navy, and Air Force.

Investments in border security, intelligence operations, and defense technology rely heavily on taxpayer contributions.

Tax revenues have made the procurement of advanced fighter jets like Rafale and the modernization of the armed forces possible.

Supporting Education and Healthcare

Access to quality education and healthcare is a fundamental right of every citizen. Tax revenue ensures the establishment and maintenance of government schools, universities, hospitals, and healthcare centers.

Example:

- **Mid-Day Meal Scheme:** Provides nutritious food to school children, improving both education and health.

- **AIIMS & Government Hospitals:** Offer medical treatment to citizens at subsidized rates or free of cost.

- **COVID-19 Vaccination Drive:** A nationwide initiative made possible through public funding.

Driving Economic Stability and Growth

Taxes help the government manage inflation, control public debt, and ensure economic stability.

Revenue from taxes is used to subsidize essential commodities such as fuel and fertilizers, support industries, and provide financial relief during economic downturns.

The introduction of the **Goods and Services Tax (GST)** has streamlined India's taxation system, reducing tax evasion and increasing revenue collection for national development.

Encouraging Financial Transparency and Compliance

Filing **Income Tax Returns (ITR)** is not just about paying taxes but also about ensuring financial credibility.

It helps individuals and businesses obtain loans, visas, and business opportunities while maintaining compliance with the law.

Businesses and individuals with a clear tax record find it easier to obtain loans, expand operations, and secure government contracts.

Promoting Social Equity and Inclusivity

India follows a progressive tax system, ensuring that higher-income groups contribute more to the economy.

This revenue is then utilized for welfare schemes, creating a more balanced society and reducing income disparity.

Example:

- The **One Nation, One Ration Card Scheme** ensures food security for migrant workers and economically weaker sections.

- Subsidies on essential services help uplift the underprivileged.

Summary

Let us summarise this in a nutshell. Paying taxes is more than just a financial obligation; it is a direct contribution to nation-building. It funds infrastructure, strengthens national security, provides education and healthcare, and ensures economic stability. Taxes play a crucial role in shaping a prosperous and self-reliant India. As responsible citizens, we must recognize that our contributions help create a better future for ourselves and future generations. After all, a strong nation is built on the active participation of its people.

"When you pay taxes, you invest in the growth of your nation."

Now, since we understand that paying taxes helps us contribute to nation-building, let us bust some myths about income tax laws.

MYTH: INCOME TAX IS THE SAME FOR EVERYONE

The burden of income tax depends on your business structure. Choosing the right business structure is crucial for tax efficiency and legal compliance. Below is a detailed analysis of different business structures along with their taxation implications. Each structure has its own benefits. The idea is to choose the structure that is optimal for running the business.

1. Sole Proprietorship

A **sole proprietorship** is a business owned and managed by an individual. It is **not a separate legal entity**, meaning the business income is treated as the individual's income.

<u>Let us understand the tax Implications.</u>

Let us cover some important tax provisions applicable to a sole proprietorship business.

Income Tax:

- Taxed under the **individual income tax slab rates** (as per the old or new tax regime).

- No separate business tax rate—profits are clubbed with the owner's income.

- No need to file a separate tax return for the business. The business income is shown under the head profit and gains from business or profession while filing the ITR.

Presumptive Taxation (Section 44AD, 44ADA & 44AE):

The **Presumptive Taxation Scheme (PTS)** under the **Income Tax Act 1961** is designed to simplify tax compliance for small businesses and professionals by allowing them to declare a fixed percentage of their turnover as taxable income.

- Eligible for **presumptive taxation** if turnover is up to ₹3 crore (for non-cash transactions).

- Under **Section 44AD**, taxable income is assumed to be **6% of turnover (digital receipts) or 8% (cash receipts)**.

- For professionals, **Section 44ADA** assumes **50% of receipts** as taxable income.

TDS & Advance Tax:

- No requirement to deduct TDS (except in specific cases).

- If tax liability exceeds ₹10,000 in a year, **advance tax** must be paid.

GST:

- If turnover exceeds **₹40 lakh (₹20 lakh for services)**, GST registration is mandatory.

- GST filing is required periodically.

Audit Requirement:

- If turnover of business **exceeds ₹1 crore** in a financial year or **₹10 crore** in case cash transaction does not exceed 5% of total transaction (for non-cash transactions) or profits are **less than 8% (or 6% digital)**, a **tax audit under Section 44AB** is required.

- Similary for specified professionals with gross receipts exceeding **₹75 lakhs,** needs to get their books audited.

2. Partnership Firm

A **partnership firm** is formed by two or more individuals agreeing to share profits and losses.

It can be **registered or unregistered**. Registration must be done with the registrar of firms in that state.

Let us understand the tax Implications.

Income Tax:

- Partnership firms are taxed at a **flat rate of 30% + 4% cess** on total income.

- **A surcharge** of 12% is applicable if income exceeds ₹1 crore.

- Income distributed to partners is **tax-free** in their hands, as it has already been taxed in the firm.

Presumptive Taxation (Section 44AD & 44ADA):

- Partnerships with a turnover **up to ₹3 crore** can opt for **presumptive taxation** (8%/6% of turnover).

- No need to maintain books of accounts or get an audit if opting for this scheme.

TDS & Advance Tax:

- **TDS deduction is mandatory** if payments exceed the prescribed limits.

- **Advance tax payment is required** if the tax liability exceeds ₹10,000 in a year.

GST & Audit Requirements:

- **GST registration is** required if turnover exceeds ₹40 lakh (₹20 lakh for services).

- **A tax audit is required if turnover exceeds ₹1 crore** (₹3 crore for presumptive taxation users). The criteria for tax audit remains same as explained in case of sole proprietor.

3. Limited Liability Partnership (LLP)

An **LLP is a hybrid structure** combining features of a partnership and a company. It has

separate legal identity from its owners and partners have limited liability.

<u>Tax Implications</u>

Income Tax:

- LLPs are taxed at a **flat rate of 30% + 4% cess.**

- **A surcharge of 12%** applies if income exceeds ₹1 crore.

- The partners' share of profit is **exempt from Tax** as LLPs pay Tax at the entity level.

Presumptive Taxation Not Allowed:

- LLPs **cannot** opt for **presumptive taxation (44AD/44ADA).**

- Must maintain proper books of accounts.

TDS & Advance Tax:

- **TDS compliance is mandatory** if payments are made beyond the prescribed limits.

- **Advance tax is required** if the liability exceeds ₹10,000 per year.

GST & Audit Requirements:

- **GST registration is required** if turnover exceeds ₹40 lakh (₹20 lakh for services).

- **Tax audit is mandatory if turnover exceeds ₹1 crore** (₹10 crore for 95% digital transactions).

4. Private Limited Company (Pvt Ltd)

A **Private Limited Company** is a **separate legal entity that limits** shareholders' liability. The Companies Act 2013 governs it.

<u>Tax Implications</u>

Income Tax:

- **New Tax Regime for Companies:**

  - **30% tax** for Domestic companies.

- **22% tax** for companies opting under **Section 115BAA** (without exemptions).

- **15% tax** for new manufacturing companies under **Section 115BAB**.

- **A 4% cess is applicable** to the Tax payable.

Dividend Distribution:

- Companies no longer pay **Dividend Distribution Tax (DDT)**.

- **Shareholders pay Tax on dividends received at** their slab rate.

MAT (Minimum Alternate Tax) – Section 115JB:

- If the company's normal Tax is **less than 15% of book profits**, then **MAT is at 15%** applies.

- Companies under **Section 115BAA/115BAB are exempt** from MAT.

TDS & Advance Tax:

- **TDS compliance is strict**—companies must deduct TDS before payments.

- **Advance tax is required** and payable in **4 installments**.

GST & Audit Requirements:

- **GST registration is mandatory** if turnover exceeds ₹40 lakh (₹20 lakh for services).

- **Mandatory statutory audit** under the Companies Act.

- **Tax audit under Section 44AB if turnover exceeds ₹10 crore (for 95% digital transactions)**.

Comparison of Taxation for Different Business Structures

Business Type	Tax Rate	Presumptive Taxation	Tax on Owner's Income	Audit Requirement
Sole Proprietorship	As per slab	Yes (44AD, 44ADA)	Yes, taxed as individual income	If turnover > ₹3 Cr (non-cash)
Partnership Firm	30% + cess	Yes (44AD, 44ADA)	Profit is tax-free, but salary/interest is taxable	If turnover > ₹1 Cr
LLP	30% + cess	No	Profit is tax-free, but salary/interest is taxable	If turnover > ₹1 Cr
Private Limited Co.	15%/22%/25%+ cess	No	Dividends are taxable for shareholders.	Mandatory

Conclusion: Choosing the Right Structure for Tax Efficiency

- **Choose Sole Proprietorship** if you have a small business with low revenue and prefer simplified compliance.

- **Choose a Partnership Firm** if you want a shared business model with tax benefits under 44AD.

- **Choose LLP** if you need **limited liability** but don't want corporate compliance.

- **Choose a Private Limited Company** if you plan to scale your business, attract investors, or want a **lower tax rate (15%- 22%)**.

MYTH: INCOME TAX IS ONLY FOR THE RICH

One of the most common misconceptions among Indian citizens is that **income tax applies only to the wealthy**. Many people believe that if they earn a modest income, they are not required to pay taxes.

However, this is not true. The Income Tax Act, 1961, mandates that anyone whose income exceeds the prescribed exemption limit must pay Tax, irrespective of whether they are considered "rich" or not.

Breaking Down the Myth

1. Income Tax Slabs Apply to Different Income Levels

The Indian income tax system follows a **progressive tax structure**, meaning tax rates increase as income levels rise.

However, taxation begins from a certain threshold, and it is not just the rich who are taxed.

Here is a comparison table of **Income Tax Slabs for Assessment Year (AY) 2025-26** under both the **New Tax Regime and Old Tax Regime**:

Income Tax Slabs for AY 2025-26 (FY 2024-25)

Income Slab (₹)	New Tax Regime (AY 2025-26)		Old Tax Regime (AY 2025-26)
Up to ₹3,00,000	Nil (No tax)	Up to ₹2,50,000	Nil (No tax)
₹3,00,001 - ₹7,00,000	5% of income exceeding ₹3,00,000	₹2,50,001 - ₹5,00,000	5% of income exceeding ₹2,50,000
₹7,00,001 - ₹10,00,000	10% of income exceeding ₹7,00,000	₹5,00,001 - ₹10,00,000	20% of income exceeding ₹5,00,000
₹10,00,001 - ₹12,00,000	15% of income exceeding ₹10,00,000	₹ Above ₹10,00,000	30% of income exceeding ₹10,00,000
₹12,00,001 - ₹15,00,000	20% of income exceeding ₹12,00,000		
Above ₹15,00,000	30% of income exceeding ₹15,00,000		

Key Differences Between the Two Regimes

Feature	New Tax Regime (AY 2025-26)	Old Tax Regime (AY 2025-26)
Basic Exemption Limit	₹3,00,000	₹2,50,000
Standard Deduction	₹75,000 (for salaried individuals)	₹50,000 (for salaried individuals)
Rebate under Section 87A	No tax if income ≤ ₹7,00,000	No tax if income ≤ ₹5,00,000
Feature	New Tax Regime (AY 2025-26)	Old Tax Regime (AY 2025-26)
Availability of Deductions (80C, 80D, HRA, etc.)	Not allowed	Allowed
Applicability	Default regime (unless opted out)	Must be specifically chosen

Which Regime to Choose?

Let's calculate the tax liability under both the **New Tax Regime** and the **Old Tax Regime** for different income levels using the correct slabs for **AY 2025-26 (FY 2024-25).**

Example 1: Income ₹9,00,000

New Tax Regime (AY 2025-26)

Standard Deduction: ₹50,000

Net Taxable Income: **₹8,50,000**

Income Slab (₹)	Tax Rate	Tax Amount (₹)
Up to ₹3,00,000	Nil	₹0
₹3,00,001 - ₹7,00,000	5%	₹20,000
₹7,00,001 - ₹8,50,000	10%	₹15,000
Total Tax Before Cess		₹35,000
4% Health & Education Cess		₹1,400
Total Tax Payable		₹36,400

Old Tax Regime (AY 2025-26) (Assuming ₹1,50,000 Deductions under 80C, 80D, etc.)

- Standard Deduction: ₹50,000

- Other Deductions (80C, 80D, etc.): ₹1,50,000

- Net Taxable Income: **₹7,00,000**

Income Slab (₹)	Tax Rate	Tax Amount (₹)
Up to ₹2,50,000	Nil	₹0
₹2,50,001 - ₹5,00,000	5%	₹12,500
₹5,00,001 - ₹7,00,000	20%	₹40,000
Total Tax Before Cess		₹52,500
4% Health & Education Cess		₹2,100
Total Tax Payable		₹54,600

Which is Better?

- **New Tax Regime Tax:** ₹36,400

- **Old Tax Regime Tax:** ₹54,600

- **The New Tax Regime is better for an income of ₹9,00,000.**

Example 2: Income ₹15,00,000

New Tax Regime (AY 2025-26)

- Standard Deduction: ₹50,000

- Net Taxable Income: **₹14,50,000**

Income Slab (₹)	Tax Rate	Tax Amount (₹)
Up to ₹3,00,000	Nil	₹0
₹3,00,001 - ₹7,00,000	5%	₹20,000
₹7,00,001 - ₹10,00,000	10%	₹30,000
₹10,00,001 - ₹12,00,000	15%	₹30,000
₹12,00,001 - ₹14,50,000	20%	₹50,000
Total Tax Before Cess		₹1,30,000
4% Health & Education Cess		₹5,200
Total Tax Payable		₹1,35,200

Old Tax Regime (AY 2025-26) (Assuming ₹2,50,000 Deductions)

- Standard Deduction: ₹50,000

- Other Deductions (80C, 80D, etc.): ₹2,50,000

- Net Taxable Income: **₹12,00,000**

Income Slab (₹)	Tax Rate	Tax Amount (₹)
Up to ₹2,50,000	Nil	₹0
₹2,50,001 - ₹5,00,000	5%	₹12,500
₹5,00,001 - ₹10,00,000	20%	₹1,00,000
₹10,00,001 - ₹12,00,000	30%	₹60,000
Total Tax Before Cess		₹1,72,500
4% Health & Education Cess		₹6,900
Total Tax Payable		₹1,79,400

Which is Better?

- **New Tax Regime Tax:** ₹1,35,200

- **Old Tax Regime Tax:** ₹1,79,400

- **The New Tax Regime is better for an income of ₹15,00,000.**

Final Comparison Conclusion

Income Level	New Regime Tax (₹)	Old Regime Tax (₹)	Which is Better?
₹9,00,000	₹36,400	₹54,600	New Regime
₹15,00,000	₹1,35,200	₹1,79,400	New Regime

Key Takeaways:

- The **New Tax Regime is better** for those who do **not** claim many deductions.

- The **Old Tax Regime is better** if deductions (80C, 80D, HRA, etc.) are **above ₹3,00,000**.

2. Exemptions and Deductions Reduce Tax Burden

The Indian tax system provides multiple deductions and exemptions under sections like **80C, 80D, 80G**, etc., allowing even middle-income individuals to **reduce their taxable income**. For example:

- **80C**: Investments in PPF, EPF, LIC premiums, and ELSS reduce taxable income by up to ₹1.5 lakh.

- **80D**: Health insurance premiums can provide tax benefits.

- **80G**: Donations to charitable institutions offer tax deductions.

Despite these benefits, people earning even slightly above the exemption threshold must file tax returns and pay applicable taxes.

3. Misconception About Salaried vs. Business Individuals

Some people assume that only **business owners or high-net-worth individuals (HNWIs)** pay Tax, while salaried individuals are exempt.

This is incorrect. **Salaried individuals, professionals, freelancers, and business owners** are all liable to pay taxes if their income exceeds the basic exemption limit.

Employers deduct **TDS (Tax Deducted at Source)** from salaried employees' incomes, ensuring compliance with tax laws.

Similarly, freelancers and business owners must calculate and pay **advance tax** based on their earnings.

4. Even Small Earners May Need to File for ITR

Even if an individual earns **below the taxable limit**, filing an Income Tax Return (ITR) is often recommended because:

- It **helps in securing loans** (banks require ITRs for approval).

- It serves as **proof of income** when applying for visas.

- Refunds can be claimed if excess TDS is deducted.

- It **prevents future scrutiny** from the tax department.

Conclusion

The notion that **income tax is only for the rich is a myth**. In reality, **anyone whose income crosses the exemption limit is liable to pay Tax**.

The system ensures fairness through progressive taxation, deductions, and exemptions. Instead of fearing taxation, individuals should focus on **proper tax planning** to minimize liability and contribute to the nation's growth.

MYTH: ITR FILING OPTIONAL IF NO TAX IS OWED

Income Tax Return Filing is Optional if No Tax is Owed – A Myth or Reality?

Many individuals believe that if their taxable income falls below the prescribed threshold, they are not required to file an Income Tax Return (ITR). While this is technically true in some cases, multiple benefits and exceptions make ITR filing essential, even when no tax is owed.

1. Understanding the Legal Requirement

According to the **Income Tax Act 1961**, individuals whose total income does not exceed the basic exemption limit are **not mandatorily required** to file an ITR. For **Assessment Year (AY) 2025-26**, the exemption limits are:

Age	Basic Exemption limit (old Regime)	Basic Exemption limit (New Regime)
Below 60	Rs. 2,50,000	Rs. 3,00,000

60 years or more but below 80 year	Rs. 3,00,000	Rs. 3,00,000
80 years and above	Rs. 5,00,000	Rs. 3,00,000

If a person's total income before deductions and exemptions does not exceed these limits, they may not be legally bound to file an ITR.

2. Cases Where ITR Filing is Mandatory Even if No Tax is Owed

There are specific situations where filing an ITR is mandatory, **even if an individual has no tax liability:**

a) If you are a company or a firm

If you are a company or a firm, filing an ITR (income tax return) is mandatory regardless of your profit or loss.

b) If TDS Has Been Deducted

Suppose **Tax Deducted at Source (TDS)** has been deducted from salary, fixed deposits, or professional earnings, but the taxable income is below the exemption limit.

In that case, an ITR **must be filed to claim a refund**.

Example:

Sneha, a freelancer, earns ₹2,40,000 in a year, but her client deducts TDS of ₹5,000. She has no tax liability, but to claim a refund of ₹5,000, she must file an ITR.

c) *If One Owns Foreign Assets or Earns Foreign Income*

Individuals who own **foreign bank accounts, foreign stocks, foreign assets, or earn foreign income** must compulsorily file an ITR, irrespective of their taxable income.

d) *If You Have Spent a High Amount on Certain Transactions*

If a person has made **high-value transactions**, filing an ITR is mandatory, even if they have no taxable income.

These include:

- Spending **₹2 lakh+** on foreign travel

- Depositing **₹50 lakh+** in a savings account

- Depositing **₹1 crore+** in a current account

- Having a total electricity bill of **₹1 lakh+** in a year

e) If You Are Carrying Forward Losses

An ITR must be filed even if no tax is payable to **carry forward business losses or capital losses** for future tax benefits.

Example:

Vikram incurred a short-term capital loss of ₹50,000 in stocks. Filing an ITR allows him to offset this loss against future capital gains.

f) If You Are a Director in a Company

If a person holds the position of **Director in a company** or has **unlisted equity shares**, they must file an ITR regardless of income.

g) If You Have Income from Crypto or Virtual Digital Assets (VDAs)

As per the latest tax laws, even if **crypto earnings are below the taxable limit**, transactions must be reported in the ITR.

h) Claiming tax exemption on capital gain

As per the Income-tax Act, an individual can claim exemption on capital gains through sections 54, 54B, 54D, 54EC, 54F, 54G, 54GA, or 54GB by filing an ITR.

The ITR filing is mandatory to claim the above exemptions.

3. Benefits of Filing an ITR Even When Not Mandatory

Even when ITR filing is **not compulsory**, it offers **several benefits: Proof of Income for Loans & Credit Cards**—Banks and financial institutions require ITR to approve home loans, car loans, and credit cards.

Visa Processing – Many countries require ITR proof for visa applications.

Avoiding Tax Notices – Filing an ITR ensures compliance and reduces the risk of receiving tax department notices.

Higher Life Insurance Coverage – Some insurers require ITR records for high-value life insurance policies.

Building Financial History – Helps in wealth planning, investment approvals, and government tenders.

Conclusion

The belief that **"Income Tax Return filing is optional if no tax is owed"** is **only partially true**. While individuals below the exemption limit are not legally required to file, many exceptions and benefits make filing an ITR a smart financial decision.

It enhances credibility, facilitates refunds, and ensures compliance with tax regulations.

Thus, even if no tax is payable, filing an ITR is **highly recommended** for financial security and future benefits.

MYTH: ITR FILING ATTRACTS TAX SCRUTINY AND RAIDS

Many taxpayers believe that filing an **Income Tax Return (ITR)** increases the risk of attracting unwanted attention from the tax authorities, leading to scrutiny or, in extreme cases, a tax raid. Although widespread, this fear is largely **unfounded**. The truth is that filing an ITR does not automatically trigger scrutiny, and it certainly does not invite a tax raid unless there are clear signs of **tax evasion or financial irregularities**.

In this chapter, we will explore the difference between **scrutiny and tax raids**, examine the real reasons behind scrutiny selection, and debunk the notion that **honest tax compliance leads to trouble**.

Understanding Tax Scrutiny vs. Tax Raid

Before addressing the myth, it is important to differentiate between two distinct actions by the Income Tax Department:

Tax Scrutiny – A standard process where the tax department **verifies the accuracy** of the return filed. It is conducted through a formal notice under **Section 143(2) of the Income Tax Act**

and does not mean wrongdoing. It is merely a check to ensure correctness. The department does this in order to ensure there is no loss of revenue to the government and that the return file is correct.

Tax Raid (Search & Seizure) – A more serious enforcement action under **Section 132**, where tax officers physically search a taxpayer's premises based on credible evidence of **tax evasion, undisclosed income, or illegal financial activities**.

Survey (Section 133A) – A softer version of a raid, often conducted at business premises to verify books of accounts.

The mere act of **filing an ITR does not lead to scrutiny or a raid**. Instead, scrutiny is triggered by **specific red flags** that indicate possible misreporting or undisclosed income.

Why Does Filing an ITR Not Increase Scrutiny?

One of the biggest misconceptions is that filing an ITR **increases the risk** of being scrutinized. However, in reality, **99% of tax returns are processed automatically without human intervention** due to advancements like **faceless assessment and artificial intelligence (AI)-based selection**. The selection of scrutiny cases is based on **predefined parameters**, not merely the act of filing an ITR.

Key Reasons Why Scrutiny Happens

Mismatch in Reported Income – If the income declared in the ITR does not match the details in Form **26AS, AIS (Annual Information Statement), or TDS records**, it may lead to scrutiny.

High-Value Transactions Without Justification – Large **cash deposits, frequent stock trading, luxury property purchases, or cryptocurrency transactions** may trigger tax scrutiny if they seem inconsistent with declared income.

Claiming Unusually High Deductions – If an individual earning ₹5 lakh claims **₹4.5 lakh in deductions under Section 80C, 80D, or HRA**, the tax department may conduct a routine verification.

Foreign Income and Assets—If an individual has **foreign bank accounts, properties, or investments** but fails to disclose them, a tax notice may result.

Business Loss Claims – Repeatedly declaring **business losses to avoid tax liability** may invite scrutiny to check the genuineness of transactions.

Thus, scrutiny is based on **data analytics and risk profiling**, not just because a taxpayer has filed a return.

Does Filing ITR Increase the Risk of a Tax Raid?

No, filing an ITR does not lead to a tax raid.

A **tax raid is an extreme step** taken only in cases where the Income Tax Department has **solid evidence** of:

- **Concealment of high-value assets**

- **Undisclosed foreign bank accounts or properties**

- **Large-scale tax evasion**

- **Benami transactions (property held under a false name)**

For instance, a salaried professional who earns ₹15 lakh per year and files regular ITRs is **not at risk of a tax raid**. However, a businessperson consistently showing **low profits but living a lavish lifestyle—owning luxury cars, multiple properties, and making heavy cash transactions—may attract scrutiny or a raid**.

In short, **a tax raid is not triggered by filing an ITR** but rather by **evidence of financial misconduct**.

Why Filing ITR is Actually Beneficial

Contrary to the myth, filing an ITR provides **numerous advantages**:

- **Smooth Loan & Visa Approvals** – Banks and embassies check ITRs as proof of financial stability before approving home loans, car loans, and visas.

- **Claiming Refunds** – If **TDS has been deducted** but no tax is actually due, an ITR must be filed to claim a refund.

- **Avoiding Penalties & Notices**—Not filing an ITR when required can result in **penalties of up to ₹10,000 and legal consequences**.

- **Better Financial Standing** – Regular ITR filing enhances **creditworthiness** for businesses and high-value investments.

Avoiding Future Scrutiny – Ironically, **not filing an ITR when required can actually increase the risk of getting a tax notice**. The tax department tracks financial transactions, and failure to file may be seen as tax evasion.

Conclusion: Filing ITR is Not a Risk; it is a Responsibility

The myth that **"filing an ITR increases the chances of scrutiny and raids"** is **completely false**. Scrutiny and raids are **triggered by suspicious financial activities, not tax compliance**.

Instead of fearing the system, taxpayers should embrace **transparent financial reporting**, ensuring that they:

- Declare their actual income accurately

- Match the figures in Form 26AS and AIS

- File their ITR on time to avoid penalties

"A well-filed return is your best defense against scrutiny." Filing ITRs not only ensures legal compliance but also brings peace of mind and financial benefits in the long run.

Cases: When Filing ITR Helped vs. When Non-Compliance Led to Trouble

Let's examine a few real-life scenarios to further emphasize the importance of filing an ITR correctly and dispel the myth of unnecessary scrutiny or raids.

Case 1: Filing ITR Prevents Scrutiny and Ensures a Smooth Loan Approval

Rahul's Story – A Young Professional Planning for the Future

Rahul, a 28-year-old software engineer, earns **₹10 lakh per annum**. Though **TDS was deducted** by his employer, he wasn't liable to pay any additional tax. Despite this, he diligently filed his ITR every year.

When Rahul applied for a **home loan**, the bank requested **the last three years' ITRs** as proof of income. Because he had filed his returns consistently, his loan was approved without any delays.

Lesson Learned: Even if no additional tax is payable, filing an ITR is crucial for financial transactions like loan approvals and visa applications.

Case 2: Late or Non-Filing of ITR Leads to Tax Notices

Sneha's Case – A Freelancer Ignoring Tax Compliance

Sneha, a freelancer earning **₹8 lakh per annum**, believed that since her TDS was already deducted, she didn't need to file an ITR. She skipped filing for two consecutive years.

A few months later, she received a **notice from the Income Tax Department** asking why she had not filed her returns despite having a taxable income.

She had to go through a long and stressful process to submit old returns, explain her income sources, and even pay a **penalty for late filing**.

Lesson Learned: Not filing an ITR, even when Tax has already been deducted, can lead to unnecessary compliance hassles and penalties.

Case 3: High-Value Transactions Without an ITR Filing Triggers Scrutiny

Amit's Case – Large Deposits Without Income Proof

Amit, a businessman, deposited **₹50 lakh in cash** into his bank account over six months but never filed an ITR, believing that "no tax owed means no filing needed."

His bank reported the transactions to the Income Tax Department under **Annual Information Statement (AIS) monitoring**. Soon, he received a notice under **Section 148** requiring him to explain the source of funds. Since he had no proper documentation, he faced **intense scrutiny, penalties, and back taxes**.

Lesson Learned: Large financial transactions without a corresponding ITR filing may raise red flags and invite unnecessary scrutiny.

Case 4: Filing an ITR Prevents Scrutiny Despite High Earnings

Priya's Case – A High-Income Professional with Transparent Finances

Priya, a senior executive earning **₹35 lakh annually**, regularly **invested in mutual funds, stocks, and real estate**. Because of her multiple income sources, she ensured her ITR was filed properly each year, matching her AIS and Form 26AS details.

Even though she made **high-value transactions**, she never faced scrutiny because her tax records were transparent, and her ITR accurately reflected her income and investments.

Lesson Learned: Higher income does not mean a higher risk of scrutiny—**accurate tax reporting ensures a hassle-free experience**.

Key Takeaways from These Cases

1. Filing ITR helps in financial transactions like loan approvals, visa applications, and credit card issuance.

2. Not filing ITR, even when no tax is owed, can lead to tax notices and penalties.

3. High-value transactions without an ITR filing can trigger scrutiny due to mismatched records.

4. Consistently filing an ITR with accurate details minimizes scrutiny risk, even for high-income individuals.

MYTH: ALL INCOME FALLS UNDER THE TAXABLE CATEGORY

Understanding the definition of income

A common question among taxpayers is whether **all income is taxable** under the **Income Tax Act 1961**. The simple answer is **no;** not all income is subject to Tax. While the tax department broadly defines "income" to include various earnings, certain categories of income are **expressly exempt from Tax** under different sections of the Act.

What is 'Income' Under the Income Tax Act?

The term' **income'** is broadly defined under **Section 2(24) of the Income Tax Act**. It includes:

- Salary, wages, and allowances

- Profits from business or profession

- Capital gains from property or investments

- Rental income from house property

- Interest from bank deposits, dividends, and other sources

- Lottery winnings, gifts, and other windfall gains

However, while most earnings are taxable, certain **specific types of income are granted exemptions** to promote social welfare, savings, and economic development.

What Income is Exempt from Tax?

The government provides **tax exemptions** on specific earnings, such as:

- Agricultural income (Section 10(1))

- Interest from Public Provident Fund (PPF) and Sukanya Samriddhi Yojana (SSY)

- Scholarships for education (Section 10(16))

- Maturity proceeds of life insurance policies (Section 10(10D))

- Gratuity received at retirement (up to prescribed limits)

- Leave encashment and Voluntary Retirement Scheme (VRS) payments

- Gifts from relatives and money received on marriage

These exemptions ensure that individuals are not taxed on **essential benefits, savings, and welfare-related earnings**.

Understanding Tax-Exempt Income in India: A Detailed Breakdown

Below is a **detailed explanation** of some of the most important exemptions available under Indian tax laws.

1. Agricultural Income (Section 10(1))

What is Agricultural Income?

Agricultural income refers to earnings from activities directly related to farming and agriculture, including:

- Rent or revenue from agricultural land

- Sale of agricultural produce without further processing, Income from farmhouses used for agricultural purposes

- Income from the primary processing of agricultural goods (e.g., drying, cleaning)

Is Agricultural Income Taxable?

- *Fully Exempt* if earned from agricultural land in India.

- *Partially Taxable* if combined with non-agricultural income and exceeds ₹5 lakh (via the partial integration method).

Example:

A farmer earns ₹8 lakh from crop sales. Since this is purely agricultural income, it is **fully tax-free**. However, if he also has a business income of ₹10 lakh, his agricultural income may be used to determine his tax slab under the **partial integration method**.

2. Interest from PPFs and Sukanya Samriddhi Yojana:

What is PPF & SSY?

Public Provident Fund (PPF): A government-backed long-term savings scheme with tax benefits.

Sukanya Samriddhi Yojana (SSY): A savings scheme for the girl child, offering tax-free returns.

Tax Benefits:

- *Contributions to PPF & SSY* – Eligible for deduction under **Section 80C** (up to ₹1.5 lakh).

- *Interest earned on PPF & SSY* – Fully **exempt from Tax**.

- *Maturity proceeds* are completely tax-free.

Example:

Rohit invests ₹1.5 lakh annually in PPF and earned ₹50,000 interest this year, which is **fully exempt from Tax**.

3. Life Insurance Proceeds (Section 10(10D))

What is Covered?

Maturity amount, bonuses, or death benefits received from a **life insurance policy**.

When is it Tax-Free?

- If the annual premium is ≤ **10% of the sum assured** (for policies issued after April 1, 2012).

- If received upon the **death of the policyholder**,

Taxable if the policy premium exceeds the prescribed limit or for certain ULIPs (as per Budget 2023).

Example:

Priya received ₹8 lakh from the maturity of her **life insurance policy**, and her premium was within the 10% rule. Her amount is **fully tax-exempt**.

4. Gratuity & Leave Encashment (Section 10(10) & 10(10AA))

A) Gratuity (Section 10(10))

Who Gets It? Employees receive a lump sum from their employer as a **retirement benefit**.

Government Employees – Fully exempt

Private Employees – The Least of the following is exempt:

- ₹25 lakh (lifetime limit)

- Actual gratuity received

- 15 days' salary × completed years of service

Example:

If Anil receives **₹20 lakh as gratuity** after 30 years of service, and his exemption limit is ₹25 lakh, the amount is **fully exempt**.

B) Leave Encashment (Section 10(10AA))

What is it? Payment for **unused paid leave** at the time of retirement or resignation.

Government Employees – Fully exempt

Private Employees – The Least of the following is exempt:

- ₹25 lakh

- 10 months' salary

- Actual leave encashment received

Example:

Rajesh, a private-sector employee, gets ₹6 lakh as **leave encashment**. Since it's within the prescribed limit, it is **fully tax-free**.

5. Gifts and Inheritance (Section 56(2)(x))

A) Tax-Free Gifts

Gifts are **exempt from Tax** if received:

- From relatives (parents, spouse, siblings, etc.)

- On marriage

- Under a Will or inheritance

Taxable If: Gifts from **non-relatives** exceed ₹50,000 in a year.

Example:

- If Neha's father gifts her **₹5 lakh**, it is **fully exempt**.

- If a friend gifts her ₹70,000, the **entire amount becomes taxable**.

B) Inheritance

Any amount received as inheritance is **fully tax-free. Example:**

Amit inherits ₹50 lakh from his grandfather. Since this is an inheritance, it is **not taxable**.

6. Scholarships & Pensions (Section 10(16) & 10(18))

A) Scholarship for Education (Section 10(16))

- Any amount received as a **scholarship for education** is fully **exempt from Tax**.

- The exemption applies **irrespective of the scholarship amount**.

Example:

Megha receives a ₹2 lakh **scholarship** for higher studies. She does **not** have to pay Tax on it.

B) Pension for Armed Forces (Section 10(18))

- **Gallantry Awardees** (Param Vir Chakra, Mahavir Chakra, etc.) – **Pension is fully exempt**.

- **Family pension** for dependents of armed forces personnel **killed in action** is also tax-free.

Example:

A widow receiving a **family pension of ₹50,000 per month** (due to her husband's service in the Army) is **not required to pay any tax** on it.

Conclusion: Why Understanding Tax-Free Income Matters

Knowing which incomes are **exempt from Tax** helps taxpayers **plan their finances**

efficiently and **legally reduce their tax burden**.

- **Maximize savings** by investing in tax-free schemes like PPF & SSY.

- **Claim rightful exemptions** for life insurance, gratuity, and scholarships.

- **Avoid unnecessary taxation** by structuring gifts and inheritance correctly.

By leveraging these **exemptions**, taxpayers can ensure **better financial planning and compliance with the law**.

MYTH: THE ITR FILING PROCESS IS OVERLY COMPLICATED

For many taxpayers, filing an **Income Tax Return (ITR)** feels like a daunting task—something best left to tax professionals. The widespread belief that the process is **too complex, time-consuming, and technical** has discouraged many individuals from filing their returns on time. But is this really the case?

Let's dispel this myth and understand how, with modern advancements, **filing ITR has become simple and hassle-free**.

Reality: Filing ITR Is Now Easier Than Ever

Gone are the days when filing an income tax return required stacks of paperwork, multiple visits to tax offices, and endless calculations. Today, the government has made significant efforts to **simplify the process**, making it accessible even to individuals with minimal financial knowledge.

Here's how filing your ITR has become **quick and straightforward**:

- **Online Filing via Income Tax Portal** – The official e-filing website (www.incometax.gov.in) offers a **step-by-step, user-friendly interface** that guides taxpayers through the process.

- **Pre-filled ITR Forms** – The portal automatically fetches details like **salary, TDS, bank interest, and investments**, reducing manual data entry and chances of errors.

- **E-Filing Tools** – The **Income Tax Department's app** allows taxpayers to **file their returns from their computer and laptop** within minutes.

- **Multiple ITR Forms for Different Taxpayers** – Individuals with **salaried income, business income, capital gains, or foreign assets** can choose the appropriate **ITR form**, making the process more structured.

- **Assistance from CA, Tax Consultants, and Online Portals**—Taxpayers can use **automated tax filing services**, many of which are **free or at minimal cost**.

Common Misconceptions About ITR Filing Complexity

"I need to understand tax laws before I can file my ITR."

No, the online system is designed to help users with little or no tax knowledge by offering easy-to-follow prompts.

"Filing ITR is a time-consuming process."

Not anymore! With pre-filled details and automated verification, it can be done in as little as 10-15 minutes.

"Mistakes in ITR lead to penalties and scrutiny."

Errors can be corrected using the 'Revised Return' option, and most minor mistakes do not lead to scrutiny unless there is deliberate fraud.

Example: Filing ITR in Just a Few Clicks

Let's take the example of **Rahul**, a salaried employee earning ₹8 lakh annually. He wants to file his ITR but is worried about the complexity. Here's how he does it in just a few steps:

⇒ **Log in to the Income Tax e-Filing Portal**

⇒ **Select "File ITR"** and choose the applicable form (**ITR-1 for salaried individuals**)

⇒ **Verify Pre-Filled Information** – His salary, TDS, and bank interest details are already auto-fetched.

⇒ **Add Any Additional Income (if applicable)** – For example, interest from FDs.

⇒ **Claim Deductions** – If eligible, he enters Section 80C deductions for EPF, LIC, PPF, etc.

⇒ **Submit & Verify Using Aadhaar OTP or Net Banking, ITR is filed successfully in minutes!**

Total Time Taken: 15 minutes

Conclusion: Filing ITR Is No Longer a Hassle

The government has made tax filing **simpler, faster, and more convenient** than ever before. Instead of seeing it as an intimidating process, taxpayers should recognize how **digital transformation has eliminated unnecessary complications**.

By embracing online tax filing, individuals can ensure **financial transparency, avoid penalties, and even benefit from tax refunds**—all with minimal effort.

So, the next time someone says, *"ITR filing is too complicated,"* you know the truth!

MYTH: INCOME TAX IS A BURDEN THAT CAN NOT BE AVOIDED

How can a salaried person Plan Income Tax Effectively?

Tax planning is an essential part of financial management that helps individuals **legally reduce their tax liability** while maximizing savings and investments. Proper tax planning ensures that you take full advantage of deductions, exemptions, and tax-saving instruments available under the **Income Tax Act 1961**.

Let's break it down into a step-by-step approach for **effective tax planning.** To start with, let us discuss the tax planning for salaried person first.

Step 1: Choose Between the Old and New Tax Regime

Understand the Difference

- The **old tax regime** offers **various deductions and exemptions** (like 80C, HRA, 80D, etc.).

- The **new tax regime** has **lower tax rates** but does **not allow most deductions.**

- If you **have significant deductions** (like 80C, 80D, home loan, etc.), the **old regime is better**.

- If you **don't have many deductions**, the **new regime may be simpler and better**.

Example:

Amit earns ₹10 lakh and has investments under **80C (₹1.5 lakh), 80D (₹25,000)**, and home loan interest (₹2 lakh).

- **Old Regime Taxable Income:** ₹6.25 lakh → Lower Tax due to deductions.

- **New Regime Taxable Income:** ₹10 lakh → Higher tax due to no deductions.

- **Best Option: The** *Old regime is better for Amit.*

Step 2: Utilize Section 80C (₹1.5 Lakh Deduction)

The most popular way to save Tax is **Section 80C**, which allows a **deduction of up to ₹1.5 lakh.**

Best 80C Investments:

- **Public Provident Fund (PPF)** – Tax-free returns, safe investment.

- **Employees' Provident Fund (EPF)** – Mandatory for salaried individuals, tax-free savings.

- **Tax-saving Fixed Deposits** – 5-year FDs are eligible under 80C.

- **National Savings Certificate (NSC)** – 5-year investment with assured returns.

- **ELSS Mutual Funds** – Equity-based mutual funds with a 3-year lock-in (best for wealth creation).

- **Sukanya Samriddhi Yojana (SSY)** – For parents of a girl child, tax-free investment.

- **Life Insurance Premium** – Premiums for term insurance or ULIPs qualify.

- **Repayment of Home Loan Principal** – If you have a **home loan**, the principal amount is deductible.

Example:

Ravi invests ₹1.5 lakh in PPF. His taxable income is reduced by ₹1.5 lakh, **saving ₹45,000 in Tax** (if in the 30% bracket).

Step 3: Get Additional Tax Deductions Beyond 80C

Apart from **80C**, here are **other deductions** that can further reduce your tax liability:

Section 80D – Medical Insurance Premium

- **Self, Spouse, Children:** Up to ₹25,000 deduction.

- **Parents (Below 60 years):** ₹25,000 extra.

- **Parents (Above 60 years):** ₹50,000 extra.

- **Maximum Deduction Possible:** ₹1 lakh (if self and parents are both senior citizens).

Example:

If Meena (30 years) pays **₹20,000 for her health insurance** and **₹40,000 for her senior citizen parents' insurance**, she can claim a **₹60,000 deduction.**

Section 24(b) – Home Loan Interest Deduction

- **Self-occupied property:** Deduction up to ₹2 lakh.

- **Rented property:** No upper limit! Full interest paid is deductible.

Example:

Amit pays **₹3 lakh as home loan interest**. He can claim a **₹2 lakh deduction under Section 24(b)**, reducing taxable income.

Additional Home Loan Benefit – Section 80EE & 80EEA

- **First-time homebuyers** can claim **₹50,000 extra** under **80EE**.

- **For affordable housing**, ₹1.5 lakh extra can be claimed under **80EEA**.

Step 4: Save Tax on Salary Components

If you are a **salaried employee**, ensure your salary structure is optimized for tax savings.

- **House Rent Allowance (HRA) Exemption** – If you live in a rented house, claim **HRA exemption** under Section 10(13A).

- **LTA (Leave Travel Allowance)** – Claim tax-free reimbursement of domestic travel expenses.

- **Food Coupons (Sodexo, Zeta, etc.)** – Tax-free up to ₹50 per meal.

- **NPS Contribution by Employer** – Deduction under Section **80CCD(2)** (in addition to 80C).

- **Car Lease Benefit** – If your employer provides a leased car, it reduces taxable salary.

Example:

Rohan gets **HRA of ₹1.2 lakh, LTA of ₹50,000**, and **food coupons worth ₹24,000**. These reduce his taxable salary, **saving ₹50,000+ in Tax**.

Step 5: Use Tax-Free Investments

- Some investment instruments **offer tax-free returns**, ensuring **maximum savings**.

- **PPF** – Completely tax-free (investment, interest, and maturity).

- **EPF** – Fully tax-free if withdrawn after 5 years.

- **Sukanya Samriddhi Yojana (SSY)** – Tax-free interest for a girl child's education.

- **ELSS Mutual Funds** – Best tax-saving investment for **higher returns**.

Step 6: Declare Investments to Your Employer

If you are salaried, submit **investment proofs** to your HR to avoid **higher TDS deductions. Deadline for investment declaration:** Usually by **January/February**.

If you **don't declare**, your employer may deduct **more Tax**, and you'll have to claim a **Refund later**.

Step 7: File Your ITR on Time

Due Date for ITR Filing:

- **Individuals & Salaried:** July 31

- **Businesses (with audit):** October 31

- **Late filing penalty:** Up to **₹5,000** (₹1,000 if income < ₹5 lakh).

Conclusion: A Smart Taxpayer is a Wealthy Taxpayer!

By following these seven **steps**, you can **save lakhs in taxes legally** while growing your wealth.

Tax planning is not just about **reducing tax liability**—it's about **building a financially secure future**.

Tax Planning For Business Owners In India

For business owners, tax planning is not just about reducing tax liability—it's about **maximizing profits, ensuring compliance, and optimizing cash flow**. Unlike salaried individuals, businesspersons have **more flexibility** in structuring their income, expenses, and investments to save taxes **legally** under the **Income Tax Act 1961**.

Let's break down a **step-by-step tax planning guide** for business owners.

Step 1: Choose the Right Business Structure

The tax liability of a business depends on its **legal structure**. Choosing the right structure can significantly impact tax savings.

Business Type	Tax Rate (AY 2025-26)	Best For
Sole Proprietorship	Same as individual tax slabs	Small businesses, freelancers
Partnership Firm	30% flat + 12% surcharge (if income > ₹1 Cr)	Small to medium businesses
LLP (Limited Liability Partnership)	30% flat + 12% surcharge (if income > ₹1 Cr)	Professional firms, consultants
Private Limited Company (Pvt. Ltd.)	22% (New tax regime)	Growth-oriented businesses

One-Person Company (OPC)	22% (New tax regime)	Solo entrepreneurs wanting limited liability

*If business profits exceed ₹10 lakh, incorporating as a **Pvt. Ltd. or LLP** can help save taxes compared to a sole proprietorship.*

Step 2: Optimize Business Expenses to Reduce Taxable Income

Under **Section 37(1)**, businesspersons can deduct **all expenses incurred for business purposes** from their income, reducing taxable profits.

Key Deductible Expenses

- **Office Rent & Utilities** – If you rent an office, the full rent is deductible.

- **Salaries & Wages** – Employee salaries, bonuses, and incentives reduce taxable income.

- **Depreciation on Assets (Section 32)** – Depreciation on machinery, vehicles, and office equipment can be claimed.

- **Marketing & Advertising Costs** – Expenses on digital ads, billboards, social media, and newspapers are **fully deductible**.

- **Professional Fees** – Fees paid to **CA, lawyers, consultants, and tax advisors** are deductible.

- **Travel & Accommodation** – If travel is business-related, flights, hotels, and local transport expenses are deductible.

- **Internet & Phone Bills** – If used for business, these are **fully deductible**.

Example:

Ravi runs an IT consulting firm and earns **₹50 lakh** per year. He incurs **₹10 lakh in business expenses** (rent, salaries, utilities).

His **taxable income reduces to ₹40 lakh**, saving **₹3 lakh+ in taxes**.

Step 3: Claim Deductions and Exemptions

1. Dedication for Business Loans (Interest Payment – Section 36(1)(iii))

- Interest on **business loans, working capital loans, and overdrafts** is **fully deductible**.

- Helps reduce **taxable income** significantly.

2. Presumptive Taxation Scheme (Section 44AD, 44ADA, 44AE)

For **small businesses, freelancers, and transporters**, the government offers **simplified taxation** with minimal compliance.

Scheme	Eligible Businesses	Taxable Income Considered	Turnover Limit
44AD	Small businesses	8% (if cash receipts) or 6% (if digital receipts) of turnover	Up to ₹3 Cr
44ADA	Professionals (Doctors, CAs, Consultants)	50% of gross receipts	Up to ₹75 lakh
44AE	Transporters (Goods Carriers)	₹1,000 per ton per month for heavy vehicles (exceeding 12000 kg) or 7500/- per month for other vehicles	Up to 10 vehicles

Example:

A consultant earning **₹50 lakh** can opt for **44ADA** and declare **₹25 lakh as taxable income.**

(50% of revenue), **saving on taxes**.

Step 4: Invest in Tax-Saving Instruments

- Business owners can use various tax-saving investments under the **Income Tax Act**:

- **National Pension System (NPS) – Section 80CCD(1B):** ₹50,000 extra deductions.

- **Health Insurance – Section 80D:** Deduct up to ₹1 lakh for self & parents.

- **Employees' Provident Fund (EPF):** Tax-free retirement savings.

- **Public Provident Fund (PPF):** Tax-free savings with an exemption on interest.

Step 5: Pay Advance Tax to Avoid Penalties

Businesspersons earning more than **₹10,000 as tax liability** must pay **advance tax** in installments.

Advance Tax Payment Schedule

Due Date	% of Tax to be Paid
15th June	15%
15th September	45%
15th December	75%
15th March	100%

Paying **advance Tax on time** helps avoid **interest under Sections 234B & 234C.**

Step 6: Maintain Proper Accounting Records

To claim deductions, businesses must maintain **proper books of account.**

- **Use Accounting Software (Tally, Zoho Books, QuickBooks, etc.)** for easy tracking.

- **Keep Receipts & Invoices** – Every expense should have proof.

- **File GST Returns Timely** – Avoid **penalties & late fees.**

A business with a turnover of ₹50 lakh+ should hire a CA to ensure tax compliance.

Step 7: Choose the Right GST Strategy

- **Opt for Composition Scheme (if turnover < ₹1.5 Cr)** – Pay a fixed **1% to 6% GST**, reducing compliance.

- **Claim GST Input Credit** – If you buy raw materials, **claim the GST paid as an input credit**, reducing tax liability.

- **File GST Returns on Time** – Late **filing leads to penalties** and ITC loss.

Example:

A manufacturer with **₹80 lakh turnover** under the **composition scheme** pays **just 1% GST**, reducing compliance and tax burden.

Step 8: File ITRs and Audit Reports on Time

Type of Business	ITR Form	Tax Audit Required?	Due Date (AY 2025-26)
Sole Proprietor	ITR-3	If turnover > ₹1 Cr (or ₹3 Cr for digital transactions)	31st July (if no audit) / 31st Oct (if audit)
Partnership Firm	ITR-5	If turnover > ₹1 Cr (or ₹3 Cr for digital transactions)	31st October
LLP & Pvt. Ltd.	ITR-6	Yes, if turnover > ₹1 Cr	31st October

A delay in ITR filing leads to a **₹5,000 late fee + interest** under Section 234F.

Conclusion: Smart Tax Planning = Higher Profits!

By following these steps, a business owner can:

- **Reduce taxable income through expenses & deductions**

- **Optimize business structure for lower tax rates**

- **Leverage tax-friendly investment options**

- **Comply with GST & advance tax rules**

A **well-planned tax strategy** ensures **higher profits, better cash flow, and financial stability.**

MYTH: HUF IS HISTORY IN MODERN TIMES

In India, one of the most effective and **legal ways to save Tax** is through a **Hindu Undivided Family (HUF)**. This unique entity is recognized under **the Income Tax Act 1961**, allowing families to **reduce their tax burden** by creating a separate tax identity.

Let's explore **how HUF works, its benefits, and how you can use it for tax planning.**

What is an HUF?

A **Hindu Undivided Family (HUF)** is a family unit that consists of A **Karta** (Head of the family) – Usually the eldest male member.

Coparceners – Sons, daughters, and grandchildren who have a right to HUF property.

Members – Other family members who can benefit from HUF income.

Who Can Create an HUF?

- HUF is available to **Hindus, Buddhists, Jains, and Sikhs.**

- It is automatically created when a Hindu family starts living together **but needs to be formally registered** for tax benefits.

How Does HUF Help in Tax Planning?

1. HUF Gets a Separate PAN & Tax Benefits

HUF is treated as a **separate legal entity** for tax purposes. This means:

- It gets a **separate PAN** and files **its own ITR**.

- It enjoys the **same income tax slab rates** as individuals.

Here is a **comparison table** of the **Old Tax Regime vs. the New Tax Regime** for **Hindu Undivided Families (HUFs) for AY 2025-26 (FY 2024-25):**

Income Tax Slabs Comparison: Old vs. New Regime

Income Range (₹)	Old Tax Regime (AY 2025-26)	New Tax Regime (AY 2025-26)
Up to ₹2,50,000	Nil (No tax)	Nil (No tax)
₹2,50,001 – ₹3,00,000	5% of income exceeding ₹2,50,000	Nil (No tax)

Income Range (₹)	Old Tax Regime (AY 2025-26)	New Tax Regime (AY 2025-26)
₹3,00,001 – ₹7,00,000	5% of income exceeding ₹2,50,000	5% of income exceeding ₹3,00,000 (Rebate under 87A available for income up to ₹7 lakh)
₹7,00,001 – ₹10,00,000	20% of income exceeding ₹5,00,000 + ₹12,500	₹20,000 + 10% of income exceeding ₹7,00,000
₹10,00,001 – ₹12,00,000	30% of income exceeding ₹10,00,000 + ₹1,12,500	₹50,000 + 15% of income exceeding ₹10,00,000
₹12,00,001 – ₹15,00,000	30% of income exceeding ₹10,00,000 + ₹1,12,500	₹80,000 + 20% of income exceeding ₹12,00,000
Above ₹15,00,000	30% of income exceeding ₹10,00,000 + ₹1,12,500	₹1,40,000 + 30% of income exceeding ₹15,00,000

Key Differences Between Old and New Tax Regime

Factor	Old Tax Regime	New Tax Regime
Basic Exemption Limit	₹2,50,000	₹3,00,000
Tax Rebate (87A) Limit	Up to ₹5,00,000	Up to ₹7,00,000
Standard Deduction	Available	Available (₹50,000)

Deductions Under 80C, 80D, etc.	Allowed	Not Allowed
HRA & LTA Exemptions	Allowed	Not Allowed
Tax Complexity	Requires documentation	Simplified

Which Regime Should You Choose?

Choose the Old Regime if:

- You claim high deductions under **80C (₹1.5 lakh), 80D (health insurance), HRA, home loan, etc.**

- You have **significant exemptions** like **LTA, HRA, and home loan interest**.

- Your taxable income after deductions is **lower than ₹7 lakh**. **Choose the New Regime if:**

- You have **fewer deductions and exemptions**.

- Your income is under ₹7 lakh (you qualify for **zero Tax under 87A**).

- You prefer a **simplified tax process** with fewer calculations.

This allows families to split income between individuals and HUF, reducing overall tax liability!

2. HUF Can Own Assets & Earn Tax-Free Income

HUF can **receive gifts and inheritances and invest** in assets like property, FDs, and stocks.

- Rental income from HUF property **is taxed separately** (not clubbed with an individual's income).

- **Tax-free gifts up to ₹50,000 per year** (beyond this, gifts from HUF members are exempt).

- Capital gains from HUF investments **are taxed separately**, reducing individual tax liability.

Example:

A father and son both earn ₹15 lakh annually. Instead of paying **30% tax each**, they create an HUF. If HUF earns ₹10 lakh in rental income, it will be **taxed separately**, allowing tax savings under lower slabs.

3. Double Deductions on Tax-Saving Investments

- HUF can claim deductions **just like individuals** under **Sections 80C, 80D, and 80G. 80C:** ₹1.5 lakh deduction for PPF, ELSS, LIC, NSC, etc.

- **80D:** Health insurance premium deduction (₹25,000 to ₹1 lakh).

- **80G:** Donations to charities qualify for deductions.

Example:

If an individual and their HUF both invest in **PPF (₹1.5 lakh each)**, they can **double their tax savings**, claiming **₹3 lakh deduction instead of ₹1.5 lakh.**

4. Business Income Can Be Diverted to HUF

- If an individual **owns a business**, part of the income can be **allocated to the HUF**, reducing overall tax liability.

- HUFs can also **hire family members**, and the salary they receive is a **deductible expense** for the HUF.

Example:

Ravi earns ₹20 lakh per year and has a family business. Instead of earning all income personally, he diverts ₹8 lakh to his **HUF account**, keeping both incomes in **lower tax slabs.**

5. HUF Can Invest & Earn Separate Tax-Free Returns

HUFs can **invest separately** in:

- **Stocks & Mutual Funds** – Gains are taxed under capital gains rules.

- **Fixed Deposits** – Interest earned is **separate from an individual's income**.

- **Rental Property** – If HUF owns the property, rental income is taxed **under HUF, not the individual**.

Example:

A HUF buys a house and earns **₹5 lakh in rental income**. Instead of being taxed under an individual's **30% bracket**, the **HUF's lower tax slabs apply**, leading to **huge tax savings**.

How to Create an HUF?

Step 1: Create an HUF Deed

- Draft a **HUF deed** stating the family members and Karta.

- Get it **stamped and notarized**.

Step 2: Apply for a PAN Card for HUF

- Fill out **Form 49A** and apply for a separate **PAN card** for the HUF.

- This is necessary for **filing taxes separately**.

Step 3: Open a Bank Account for HUF

- A separate **HUF bank account** must be opened.

- All income, gifts, and business transactions should be conducted through this account.

Step 4: Transfer Assets & Start Investing

- HUF can **receive gifts, property, and investments** from members.

- Start investing in tax-free instruments like **PPF, ELSS, and real estate**.

Important Rules and Limitations of HUF

HUF Income Cannot Be Easily Divided – Once an income is assigned to HUF, it **belongs to the family** and cannot be taken back as individual income.

HUFs Can't Be Created Just for Tax Evasion—The IT Department monitors **artificial HUFs** created just to reduce taxes.

HUF Can't Have Salaried Income – A salaried person **cannot shift their salary** to a HUF for tax benefits.

Partitioning an HUF is Irreversible – Once dissolved, an HUF **cannot be restarted** with the same assets.

Conclusion: Is HUF a Good Tax Planning Tool?

- **Yes, if you have multiple income sources** (business, property, investments).

- **Yes, if you want to reduce tax liability legally**.

- **Yes, if you want to create long-term family wealth** through tax-free investments.

- **Not useful for salaried individuals** with no other sources of income.

By using **HUF strategically**, families can **legally save lakhs in taxes** while ensuring financial security for future generations.

MYTH: I DON'T NEED TO PAY TAX WHEN I SELL LAND, BUILDING, OR SHARES

Let us understand the Capital Gain Provisions under the Income Tax Act.

Capital Gain refers to the **profit earned** from the sale of a **capital asset** such as land, buildings, stocks, mutual funds, gold, or other investments. It is classified into **two types** based on the holding period:

1. **Short-Term Capital Gain (STCG)** – When the asset is held for a short duration before being sold.

2. **Long-Term Capital Gain (LTCG)** – When the asset is held for a longer duration before sale.

The **Income Tax Act 1961** has different tax rates, exemptions, and rules for STCG and LTCG.

1. Classification of Capital Assets

A **Capital Asset** includes:

- **Immovable Property** – Land, buildings, house property.

- **Movable Property** – Jewelry, paintings, sculptures, etc.

- **Financial Assets** – Stocks, mutual funds, bonds, debentures.

- **Cryptocurrency** – Considered a capital asset under Section 115BBH (taxed separately).

Exceptions: The following are **not considered capital assets**:

- Stock-in-trade (business inventory)

- Personal movable items(Clothes, furniture, vehicles etc)

- Agricultural land in rural areas

2. Holding Period for Capital Gains Classification

Type of Asset	Short-Term (STCG)	Long-Term (LTCG)
Equity shares, equity mutual funds, listed securities	Held for ≤ 12 months	Held for > 12 months
Debt mutual funds, gold, bonds, real estate	Held for ≤ 24 months	Held for > 24 months
Immovable property (land & buildings)	Held for ≤ 24 months	Held for > 24 months
Type of Asset	Short-Term (STCG)	Long-Term (LTCG)
Unlisted shares	Held for ≤ 24 months	Held for > 24 months

When it comes to *Crypto & Virtual Digital Assets (VDA), they are taxed at a fixed 30% rate, regardless of holding period.*

3. Tax Rates on Capital Gains

Short-Term Capital Gains (STCG) Tax Rates

- STCG on listed equity shares & equity mutual funds (where STT is paid): 15% (under Section 111A)

- STCG on other assets (real estate, gold, debt funds, unlisted shares, etc.): Taxed as per income tax slab rates

Long-Term Capital Gains (LTCG) Tax Rates

- **LTCG on listed equity shares & equity mutual funds** (where STT is paid):

  - **10% on gains exceeding ₹1 lakh (under Section 112A)**

  - No indexation benefit is allowed.

- **LTCG on real estate, unlisted shares, gold, and debt funds:**

  - 20% with indexation benefit (under Section 112)

  - 12.5% (effective from July 23, 2024)

Indexation adjusts the purchase price for inflation, reducing taxable capital gains.

4. Calculation of Capital Gains

Short-Term Capital Gain Formula

$$STCG = \text{Sale Price} - (\text{Purchase Price} + \text{Transfer Expenses} + \text{Improvement Cost})$$

Tax is applied based on the **type of asset** (15% for listed shares, slab rate for others).

Long-Term Capital Gain Formula

$$LTCG = \text{Sale Price} - (\text{Indexed Purchase Price} + \text{Transfer Expenses} + \text{Improvement Cost})$$

Indexed Purchase Price = **Purchase Cost × (CII of Sale Year / CII of Purchase Year)**

Where **CII (Cost Inflation Index)** is notified by the government annually.

5. Exemptions on Capital Gains

Certain exemptions are available to **reduce or eliminate capital gains tax**:

Section 54: Exemption for Sale of Residential Property

Condition: Invest the LTCG amount in another **residential property** within **2 years (purchase) or 3 years (construction).**

Limit: Only available for **individuals & HUFs.**

Restriction: You cannot claim for more than **two properties.**

Section 54F: Exemption for Sale of Any Asset Other than a House

Condition: You must invest the **entire sale proceeds** (not just gains) in a new residential property.

Restriction: You cannot own more than **one house before the sale.**

Section 54EC: Exemption for Sale of Land or Building

Condition: Invest LTCG in **specified bonds (NHAI, REC, PFC, IRFC) within 6 months.**

Limit: Maximum ₹50 lakh investment allowed. **Lock-in period: 5 years.**

6. Special Cases of Capital Gains Taxation

Capital Gains on Property Sale (TDS Implications)

- If a property is sold for more than ₹**50 lakh**, the buyer must deduct **1% TDS** under

Section 194IA.

- If the seller is an **NRI**, TDS is deducted at **20% on LTCG** (plus surcharge & cess).

Capital Gains on Mutual Funds

- **Equity Mutual Funds (LTCG > ₹1 lakh):** 10% tax (Section 112A).

- **Debt Mutual Funds (from April 1, 2023): Fully taxable as per slab rate** (no indexation benefit).

Capital Gains on Gifts & Inheritance

- **Gifted assets:** No capital gains tax **at the time of the gift**, but when the recipient sells the asset, gains are calculated based on the **original purchase price** of the donor.

- **Inherited assets:** No tax on inheritance, but LTCG applies when the asset is sold.

7. **Set-Off and Carry Forward of Capital Losses**

- **Short-term capital losses (STCL)** can be **set off against** both **STCG & LTCG.**

- **Long-term capital losses (LTCL)** can be **set off only against LTCG**.

- **Unutilized capital losses** can be **carried forward for 8 years** and adjusted against future gains.

Losses cannot be set off against salary, business income, or other sources.

8. Recent Amendments and Important Updates

Crypto Taxation (Section 115BBH)

- Flat 30% tax on gains from cryptocurrency and digital assets.

- No set-off of losses against any other income.

- TDS of 1% on transactions exceeding ₹50,000 (₹10,000 for certain individuals).

Taxation of Debt Mutual Funds (from April 1, 2023)

- **Debt funds are now taxed as per individual slab rates**, removing LTCG benefits.

New TDS on Property Sales by NRIs

- If an NRI sells the property, **TDS is deducted at 20% (LTCG) or as per the slab (STCG).**

- NRIs can apply for **lower TDS certificates** from the IT department.

Conclusion

Capital gains taxation is an essential part of financial planning. Knowing **how different assets are taxed** and using **legal exemptions** can help you **reduce tax liability and maximize savings**.

OTHER COMMON MYTHS OF INCOME TAX LAW

Myth: Gifts Received are Always Tax-Free

Reality: Gifts are **taxable under the "Income from Other Sources"** section unless:

- They are received from **relatives** (parents, siblings, spouse, etc.).

- They are below ₹50,000 in a financial year.

- They are received on special occasions like a **marriage**.

Myth: Women Have Different Tax Slabs Than Men

Reality: There are no separate tax slabs for women in India.

The tax structure is the same for both men and women, but they can **claim deductions** on home loans, investments, and savings schemes just like men.

Myth: TDS Deduction Means No Need to File ITR

Reality: TDS (Tax Deducted at Source) is **only a partial tax payment.** You must still file an ITR to:

- **Claim a refund** if excess TDS was deducted.

- **Report all sources of income** correctly.

- **Adjust tax liability** based on your total income.

Myth: ITR Can't Be Filed After the Due Date

Reality: If you miss the ITR deadline, you can still file a **belated return** (with penalties) until **December 31 of the assessment year**.

However, you won't be able to carry forward losses or claim certain refunds.

Myth: NRIs Do Not Have to Pay Tax in India

Reality: Non-Resident Indians (NRIs) **must pay Tax in India** on:

- Income earned or received **in India** (such as rental income, dividends, or capital gains).

- Interest earned on **NRO (Non-Resident Ordinary) accounts**.

NRIs should check **DTAA (Double Taxation Avoidance Agreements)** to avoid paying Tax twice.

Myth: Cash Transactions are Not Taxable

Reality: Cash income is **not exempt from Tax**. The Income Tax Department monitors

high-value cash deposits, withdrawals, and property transactions.

- Cash deposits over **₹10 lakh in a savings account** in a year are reported to the IT department.

- **Property transactions over ₹30 lakh** are flagged for scrutiny.

Myth: Lottery Winnings and Game Show Prizes Are Tax-Free

Reality: Prize money from **lotteries, game shows, and contests** is taxable at **a flat 30% under Section 115BB**, with no deductions allowed.

Myth: Paying Tax Once Means No Need to Pay Again Next Year

Reality: Income tax is **calculated and paid annually** based on the **previous financial year's income**.

Taxpayers must **file returns every year,** even if their tax liability remains the same.

Myth: If I Don't File ITR, The IT Department Won't Notice

Reality: The Income Tax Department has **data tracking mechanisms** such as **Form 26AS, AIS (Annual Information Statement), and PAN-based tracking** to monitor:

- High-value transactions

- Property and car purchases

- Large credit card spending

If your income is taxable but you haven't filed an ITR, you may receive a **tax notice**.

Myth: I Can File ITR Anytime Without Penalty

Reality:

- The **due date for filing ITR is July 31** (unless extended).

- Late filing attracts **a penalty of up to ₹5,000** under **Section 234F**.

- You **cannot carry forward losses** if the ITR is filed late.

Myth: Filing ITR Once Makes It Mandatory Every Year

Reality: ITR filing is based on income, not past filings.

If your income is **below the taxable limit in a financial year**, you are **not required** to file an ITR. However, filing it voluntarily can help maintain financial records.

Myth: If I Have Multiple PAN Cards, I Can Avoid Taxes

Reality: Holding **multiple PAN cards is illegal** and can lead to:

- **Penalty of ₹10,000 under Section 272 B.**

- **Possible blocklisting by the Income Tax Department.**

- **Difficulty in financial transactions.**

Always use **only one PAN card** and update details if required.

Myth: Only Large Transactions Are Tracked by the Income Tax Department

Reality: The IT department tracks both **high and unusual transactions**, such as:

- Deposits over ₹10 lakh in savings accounts.

- Credit card payments above ₹1 lakh in cash.

- Buying property worth ₹30 lakh+.

Even small cash transactions can be flagged if they don't match declared income.

Myth: Fixed Deposit (FD) Interest is Not Taxable

Reality: FD interest is **fully taxable** under "Income from Other Sources":

- Banks deduct **TDS at 10% if interest exceeds ₹40,000 (₹50,000 for seniors).**

- If total taxable income is below the exemption limit, you can **file Form 15G/15H to avoid TDS.**

Myth: Life Insurance Maturity Proceeds are Always Tax-Free

Reality: Maturity proceeds are **only tax-free if:**

- The **premium paid is less than 10% of the sum assured.**

- The policy follows **Section 10(10D) conditions.**

High-premium ULIPs and policies exceeding limits may be **taxable under Section 194DA.**

Myth: Selling Shares After One Year is Completely Tax-Free

Reality: Long-term capital gains (LTCG) on equity shares and mutual funds **above ₹1.25 lakh** are taxed at **12.5% under Section 112A.**

Thank You for Reading

Unmasking Income Tax Myths

By

CA Ritesh Pal

Scan the QR code below to leave your valuable feedback.

Thank You!